Creative Mind

CREATIVE MIND

Updated and Gender-Neutral

* * *

Ernest Holmes

newt
LIST

Chicago • New York

CONTENTS

Part 1
Analysis of Contents
1

Part 2
Practice
71

Contents

Part 1

Analysis of Contents

IN THE BEGINNING

*　*　*

"In the beginning, God!" The words are clear and expressive. In the beginning, God only. No manifest universe. No system of planets. Nothing of form or life, of brute or human. God was the Spirit of all that was to be, but God had not yet moved on the waters.

Then, the Spirit moved; it began to create. But to where did Spirit move? On what did it create? Where did it get the pattern? What means or power did it employ? Through what agencies did it work? In short, what is the world—ourselves included—made out of, and how did we and all else come into being? These questions correctly answered would solve the problem of existence and set all people free.

In the beginning, Spirit was all. There was nothing else but itself. All-inclusive, everywhere, infinite. This all-Spirit could not have had the impulse to move unless it was self-conscious. Therefore, the Spirit is the power that knows itself. It is accordingly all-knowing as well as all-present. Being one and undivided, whatever it knows, it knows everywhere instantly. Spirit operates through self-knowing. It moves, and that inner movement must be one of infinite power moving upon itself with a definite purpose. The Spirit, then, moves on itself and makes out of itself all that is made. In other words, what we see comes from what we do not see, through some inner intelligence at work that knows there is no power but itself. "The things that are seen are not made of the things that do appear."

The only possible operation of intelligence is thought, or *the word*. All things were made by the word, and "without the word was not anything made that has been made." The process of creation is so simple when we understand it. The Spirit speaks, and since there is nothing but the Spirit, and it is all-power, it has only to speak and it is done. "The word was with God, and the word was God."

From the word, then, comes forth all that appears. Each life, human or divine, each manifestation, is a different kind of word coming into expression. The great fact to dwell on is that Spirit needs nothing to help it. It is self-conscious and has all power and all ability to do whatever it wishes to accomplish. It operates simply by speaking.

It is hard to get a clear concept of this great ceaseless cause, this thing from which all things come. At times, we fall into a maze of confusion when we attempt to realize what Spirit means. At these times, we should think of Spirit as the great reason behind everything. Being all-knowledge, it must know itself and must know everything it creates. So it knows us, and it knows everyone. Since it is all-presence, we can contact it anywhere. We never have to go to some particular spot to find it. As it is all-knowing and operates through the power of the word, it knows everything we think. Just how it creates, we cannot know and need not attempt to understand, because whatever this process of creation is, we find it is always an inner thought process.

We should always remember that Spirit makes all things out of itself. Everything comes into being without effort, and when we exert ourselves, we are not in accord with the creative Spirit in the way it works. The impulse of Spirit to move must be caused by a desire to express what it feels itself to be—beauty, form, color, life, love, and power. All other things that we find in the manifest universe are attributes of the Spirit and are caused to spring into existence through the word, because Spirit wants to enjoy itself.

We find, then, that the word, which is the inner activity of thought, comes first, and all else comes from the effect of the word operating on a universal substance. If the word precedes all else, then the word is what we are looking for, and when we get it, we will have what the world has sought from time immemorial. We must, if we wish to prove the power of the Spirit in our lives, look not to outside things or effects, but to the word alone.

The human eye sees and the human hand touches only that which is an effect. Unseen law controls everything, but this law is also an effect. Law did not make itself. The law is not intelligence or causation. Before there can be a law, there must be something that acts, and the law is the way it acts. It is intelligence.

"In the beginning was the word." This word, or activity of the Spirit, is the cause of the law. The law in its place is the cause of the thing, and the thing is always an effect. It did not make itself; it is a result. The word always comes first. "The word was with God, and the word was God," and the word still is God.

When we realize that the individual is like God (and the individual could not be otherwise, since it is made out of God), we realize that each person's word also has power. If there is only one mind, then it follows that our word, our thought, is the activity of that one mind in our consciousness.

The power that holds the planets in place is the same power that flows through humankind. We must place the word where it belongs, whether it is the word of God in the universe or the word of the human in the individual. It is always first, before all else, in the beginning. The real sequence is this: First, there is cause, Spirit, intelligence, God; and second, the word, the activity of intelligence, the effect, the visible thing. Whether it is a planet or a peanut, everything is made out of the same thing.

We need to learn how to use the word so that all people come to see that they are creative centers within themselves.

A Principle That Can Be Proven

* * *

Knowing that mind *is*, we have a principle that is absolute. It is exact. It is going to correspond to our thinking about it. The first great necessity is to believe this. Without belief, we can do nothing. This is the reason Jesus said, "It is done unto you even as you have believed." Always, it is done unto us as we believe, and there is something that does it that never fails.

We must believe that our word is formed on and around this creative mind. For instance, suppose we wish to create activity in our business. When we believe that our word is law about our business, something takes our thought and executes it for us. If we have accepted the fact that all is mind and that the thought is the thing, we will see at once that our word is the power behind the thing and that it depends on the word, or thought, that we are sending out.

Mind is so plastic and receptive that the slightest thought makes an impression on it. People who think a multiplicity of thoughts must expect to receive a confused manifestation in their lives. If a gardener plants a thousand types of seeds, a garden will grow a thousand kind of plants. It is the same in mind.

THE WORD GOING FORTH

*   *   *

Everything depends on our mental concepts. "As one thinks in one's heart, so it is." The Bible reiterates this statement, telling us many times of the creative power of thought. Jesus taught nothing else. He said, "The words which I speak unto you, they are Spirit and they are life."

The centurion coming to Jesus recognized the power of the word spoken by Jesus. The centurion said, "I also am one in authority." His authority was on the physical plane, but he saw that Jesus had authority on a spiritual plane, because he said, "Speak the word only."

The Bible tells us that the word is not far off, but in our own mouths. It is neither here nor there; it is within every living soul. We must take responsibility for our own lives. We must wake up to the knowledge that we have absolute control over our lives and that nothing can happen by chance. Then, we will have a broader concept of God, a greater tolerance for our neighbor, and a greater realization of our divine nature. What a relief from strenuous labor! No more struggle or strife. "Be still and know that I am God, and beside me there is none other."

Knowing that Spirit is all there is, we cannot conceive of anything that can hinder its working. When the Spirit has spoken, the word becomes law, because the law comes before the word. It precedes all else. First is absolute intelligence, all-power, all-presence, all-causation; then, the movement upon itself through the power of the word; next, the word becoming law; and finally, the law producing the thing and holding it in place.

As long as the word exists, the thing will exist. Since the word is all-power, there is nothing except it. "I am that I am, and beside me there is none other." This *I am* is Spirit, God, all. There is no physical explanation for anything in the universe. All causation is Spirit, and all effect is spiritual. We are not living in a physical world, but in a spiritual world peopled with spiritual ideas. We now live in Spirit.

God, or Spirit, governs the universe through mental laws that work out the divine will and purpose, always operating from intelligence. The intelligence is so vast and the power is so great that our human minds cannot even grasp it. All we can hope to do is to learn something of the way in which it works and, by harmonizing ourselves with it, to so align ourselves with Spirit that our lives may be controlled by the great harmony that obtains in all the higher laws of nature yet has been imperfectly manifested in humankind.

WHY AND WHAT IS HUMANKIND?

*   *   *

In the physical universe, automatic laws govern everything. For instance, the tree cannot say, "I will not" because of the law that holds it in place. It grows without any volition of its own. That is how it is in nature. But when we come to humankind, we find a different manifestation of the Spirit. The individual is a being who can say, "I choose." In all creation, humankind alone is an individual. Humankind alone is free, and yet it wants, is sick, suffers, and is unhappy. Humankind marks the earth with ruin. Why? Because it has not found its true nature. The very thing that should free us, and eventually will do so, now limits us. God could not make us without giving us the ability to think, and we cannot think without bringing on ourselves the results of our thought, good or bad. This does not mean using two powers, but using the one from two standpoints. Nothing in itself is either good or bad; all things exist in mind as a potentiality. Mind is eternally acting on thought, continually producing its own images from itself and casting them out into manifestation. Humankind must be the outcome of the desire of the Spirit to make something that expresses the same life that it feels. We are made to be companions of the infinite. To arrive at this exalted plane of being, though, we must have our freedom and be let alone to discover our own nature, to return love to our creator only when we choose to do so. At the doorway of the individual's mind, then, this wonderful God has to wait. "Behold, I stand at the door and knock." The opening must be on the part of the individual.

We live in a mind that presses in on us from all sides with infinite possibilities, with infinite creative power. The divine urge of infinite love crowds itself upon us and waits for our recognition. Being the image of this power, our thought also must be the word, or cause, in life. At the center of our being is all the power we will need on the path of our unfoldment. The total sum of the mind we possess is the total sum of infinite mind that we allow to flow through us. We have often thought of God as distant and of humankind as being separate from it.

Now, we see that God and humankind are one and that Spirit is simply waiting for our recognition, so that we all may spring into being and become to humanity all that we could wish or want. "As parents have inherent life in themselves, so have they given to the children to have life within themselves." It could not be otherwise. We are all in mind, and mind is always creating for us as we think. Since we are constantly thinking creatures, our happiness depends on our thoughts.

THE LAW OF OUR LIVES

* * *

Spirit creates through law. The law is mind in action. Mind cannot act unless intelligence sets it in motion. In the great universal mind, the individual is the center of intelligence, and every time we think, we set mind into action. What is the activity of this mind in relation to a person's thought? It has to be one of mental correspondence. Mind must reflect whatever thought is cast into it. Wonderful as universal mind is, it has no choice but to create whatever thought is given it. If it could contradict a thought, it would not be one entity, because this would be recognizing something outside itself. This is an important point. The one mind knows only its own ability to make whatever is given it. It sees no other power and never analyzes or dissects. It simply *knows*, and the reason why we do not understand this is that we have not realized what mind is. Ordinary individuals think of mind only from the limitation of their own environment. The concept they have of mind is the concept of their own thinking, which is very limited.

We are surrounded by an all-seeing, all-knowing mind, which is one and runs through all. The belief in the dual mind has destroyed many philosophies and religions, and will continue to do so until the world comes to see that there is only one. Whatever name we give it, it is still one. It is this one that creates for us whatever we believe. Our thought, operative through this one, produces all our affairs. We are each a center in this mind, a center of creative thought activity. There is nothing that appears in the manifest universe other than an objectified thought, whether it is a bump on your head or a planet in space. Nothing could exist if it were not made out of mind, because mind is all there is to make anything out of. Whatever exists is made out of it. Nothing exists or can exist without a source from which it springs.

We are not dealing with a negative as well as a positive—not two powers, but one. It is a power that sees neither good nor evil as we see it. It knows only that it is all. Since it is all, it creates whatever is given it. From our limited standpoint, we often think in terms of good and evil, not realizing that, as yet, we do not know the one from the other. What we call good today, we may call evil tomorrow, and what we think to be evil today, we may tomorrow proclaim as the greatest good we have known. Not so with the universal power of mind. It sees only itself and its infinite ability to create.

It is important for us to see that we are no longer living in a limited universe, a world of powers, but that we are immersed in an infinite creative medium that, because of its nature, has to create for us whatever we believe. Jesus understood this and laid down the law of life in a few simple words: "It is done unto you as you believe." This is a great thing to keep in mind. It is done unto us. We do not have to do it, because it is done unto us of a power that knows itself to be all there is. If we believe that an actual mountain could be moved, the power is there to do it. Without this belief, there is no real impulse for the creative mind and we do not get an affirmative answer. We must realize more clearly that this great power must operate through us.

THE INDIVIDUAL'S PART

❋   ❋   ❋

Creative mind cannot force itself on us, because we have the power of self-choice. It recognizes us when we recognize it. When we think that we are limited or have not been heard, the one mind must take that thought and bring it into manifestation for us.

Sometimes when we observe nature so beautiful, lavish, and limitless, we realize that a power of abundance is the source of everything and that there exists more than could be used. At the same time, though, we sometimes see humankind as being limited, sick, sad, and needy. At these times, we might ask these questions: Is God good? Does God really care for the people of God's creation? Why am I sick? Why am I poor? Little do we realize that the answer is in our own mouths, in the creative power of our own thought. Yet, when told the truth, the average person will still seek some other way.

God has already done for us all that it can do. Having been given the ability, we have to do the rest for ourselves. The power is always near, ready at any time to help, but we must use it according to its own nature, in harmony with its laws. We must learn that each one of us is a center of this divine activity. Realizing this, we must seek more and more to utilize our own divine natures. By doing so, we will come more fully under the protection of the laws that govern all life, manifest and unmanifest.

Whatever we are, we must find that. Since we are made out of God, we are of the same nature. The infinite one cannot know anything outside of itself or anything that would be a contradiction of its divine nature. Ignorance of our real nature binds us with our own freedom until we come to see things as they really are and not as they appear to be.

In the infinity of mind, which is the principle of all life, there is nothing but mind and that which mind does. That is all there is in the universe. That is all there ever was or ever will be. This mind is acted on by our thought, and so our thought becomes the law of our lives. It is just as much a law in our individual lives as God's thought is in the larger life of the universe.

For the sake of clarity, think of yourself as in this mind, as a center in it. That is your principle. You think, and mind produces the thing. One of the main points to remember is that you do not have to create. All you have to do is to think. Mind—the only mind that there is—creates.

Few people seem to understand the nature of the law. They think that they have to do something, even if it is only to hold a thought. Thinking or knowing is what does the thing. It will make it much easier for us when we realize that we do not have to make anything. We just to have to *know*. There is something behind the knowing that does the work for us.

We get the best results when we realize that we can use this divine principle. When we can achieve the clearest concept of our idea, we can rely on mind to do the rest for us, keeping everything out of our thoughts that would contradict the supremacy of Spirit, or mind.

By simply holding a thought, we could not make anything, but by knowing in mind, we can do everything.

BONDAGE AND FREEDOM

* * *

Never get away from the fact that you are surrounded by such a power. It is the principle of demonstration. It knows every thought. As we send our thoughts into it, it does unto us. Those who are ignorant of this law must, by that ignorance, be bound by their thought, by their human beliefs. Those who understand will begin to break these ties that bind them. One by one, they will destroy every negative thought until at last they are able to think what they want to think. They will free themselves by the use of the same power that at one time bound them.

We must destroy all thought that we do not want to see manifest and hold to that which we want to see, until we receive the affirmative answer.

27

Never struggle. Mind makes things out of itself. There is no effort made. Don't think that there is a lot to be overcome. Have only a calm sense of perfect peace as you realize that God is all, that you are using the perfect law, and that nothing can hinder it from working for you. Many people are learning to do this, and no one who is steadfast will fail to demonstrate it when they use the law with a consistent and persistent trust.

All that we have to do is to provide the right mental and spiritual attitude of mind and believe that we already have, and then the reward will be with us. We will see it.

The time will come when we will not have to demonstrate at all because we will be always living so near to the law that it will do everything for us without much conscious thought on our part.

When we say, "I am poor, sick, or weak" or "I am not one with the creative mind," we are using that creative power to keep ourselves away from the infinite. Just as soon as we declare that we are one with God, there is a rushing out to meet us, just as the parent rushed out to meet the prodigal. "The Spirit seeks," but as long as our mind thinks in the terms of conditions, we cannot overcome. The difficulty comes from our inability to see our own divine nature and its relation to the universe. Until we wake up to the fact that we are one in nature with God, we will not find the way of life. Until we realize that our own word has the power of life, we will not see the way of life.

THE WORD

* * *

"The word was with God, and the word was God."
"The word is near you, even in your own mouth, that
you should know it and do it." What does this mean? It
clearly states that the power that is in the word, which it
says is all power, is also in our own mouths.

There is no avoiding the fact that the Bible claims for
us the same power in our own lives and our world that
it claims for God. In the lives of the majority, we do not
realize that the word is in our own mouths. What word?
Little do we realize that this word we are so earnestly
seeking is every word we hear, think, or speak. Do we
who are endeavoring to realize the greater truths of life always govern our words? If any word has power, it follows

that all words have power. It is not in the few moments of spiritual meditation that we demonstrate, but we bring out the possibilities of the hidden word each time we allow our thoughts to run in any direction.

We are always using the word, not only in the short time spent in prayer, but also in the long hours stretching themselves into days, months, and years. An hour a day spent in silent meditation will not save us from the confusion of life. The fifty-one percent of our thinking is what counts.

When we are alone, it can be easy to brave the storms of life. Surrounded by our own exalted atmosphere, we feel the strength of the infinite. We rise in Spirit and think we are experiencing the ultimate of truth, that all things are ours. These moments in a busy life are well spent but must unavoidably be brief. So, what of the rest of the day? What of the busy street, of the grocery store, of all the daily contact with life? Do we obtain then? Do we keep on in the same, steady way? Or do we fall before the outer confusion of our surroundings? We are always creating the word and setting it afloat in the great ethers of life. Are these words creating for us? Yes!

How necessary, then, to "keep the independence of the solitude," and how seldom we do this.

Few people today are well poised. Where do we find those who can live above their surroundings, who in their own thoughts can dominate all conditions and, in the midst of the crowd, keep their own way and their own counsel? When we do meet with such people, we will know them, because we will find the image of perfect peace on their faces. We will detect in their bearing the ease and independence that come only to those who have found themselves and who are centered not in the outer, but in the inner world.

People like this have the power to attract to themselves all of the best in the world. They are centers toward which all else must gravitate. The atmosphere that they create and with which they surround themselves is one of absolute calm and peace. The world at once sees these people as masters and gladly sits at their feet.

Yet, those who have risen above the thought of the world care not that other people should sit at their feet. They know that what they have done, all may do, and they know that all the teaching in the world will not produce another such as them. They know that it is not from the teaching, but from the being, that true greatness springs. These people do not go around teaching or preaching. They simply *are*.

THE INDIVIDUAL WHO HAS ARRIVED

* * *

Those who have arrived will realize that they have done so in the midst of an outer confusion. They will be the ones who have gone into the silence for strength and have come back into the world equipped with power from on high. But the light that they have received must be kept burning.

Not alone in the silence, but in the busy throng must all of us find the way of life. Our every thought creates. For the majority of us, these thoughts come in everyday affairs. Some of these are trivial, yet they too will be demonstrated.

We have missed the whole point unless we have learned to control our thought so that time and place make no difference.

THE POWER WITHIN US

*   *   *

We have a power within that is greater than anything that we will ever contact in the outer, a power that can overcome every obstacle in our life and make us safe, satisfied, and at peace, healed and prosperous in a new light and in a new life.

Mind—all mind—is right here. It is God's mind, God's creative power, God's creative life. We have as much of this power to use in our daily lives as we can believe in and embody.

Nature is filled with infinite good, waiting for the touch of our awakened thought to spring forth into manifestation in our life, but the awakening must be on our part and not on the side of life.

We stand at the gateway of limitless opportunity in the eternal and changeless now. Today is the day in which to begin a new life that is to lift us up to the greater expression of all that is wonderful. The word that we speak is the law of our life, and nothing hinders it but ourselves. We have, through ignorance of our real nature, misused the power of our word, and this has brought on us "the very thing that we feared." But now it will produce a new thing, a new heaven and a new earth.

Individual Ideas

* * *

We find that every idea in the universe has a mental concept, or *word*, behind it. As long as that concept remains, the idea is held in place in the visible world. When the concept is withdrawn, the idea melts away and disappears. It ceases to vibrate to the concept, which is the law behind it, because when the concept is withdrawn, the condensation of the atmosphere that forms the concept melts again into the formless.

There was a time when the world was without form, and from the word alone all things were made. When our word says that there is no longer life in our bodies, the life principle withdraws and our body returns to the substance from which it came. Here is the great mystery of life: We are able to use our creative word for whatever purpose we may desire, and our word becomes the law unto the thing for which it is spoken.

We might say that without our word was not anything made in our lives, because we are given the power to sit in the midst of our lives and direct all of our activities. There is no struggle and no strife necessary. All that we have to do is to know. We must wake up and, with the glorified consciousness of an emancipated soul, use our God-given power.

THE REASON FOR THE UNIVERSE

* * *

The universe is the reason of an infinite intelligence that speaks or thinks. As this thought becomes active within itself, it creates from itself, at the power of its own word, the visible universe.

We are living in a universal activity of mental law. We are surrounded by a mind that receives every impression of our thought and returns to us just what we think. All individuals, then, are living in a world made for them from the activity of their thoughts.

It is a self-evident proposition that mind must create out of itself. This self being limitless, it follows that its creative power is without limit.

Mind in Action

* * *

Everything that we see is the result of mind in action. We each have a body and we each have a physical environment. We could have neither if it were not for mind. The law implanted within us is that we need only ourselves and this all-wise creative mind to make anything. As long as we depend on any condition, past, present, or future, or on any individual, we are creating chaos, because we are dealing with conditions and not with causes.

All living souls are laws unto themselves, but few people are conscious of this great truth. It seems difficult for the human race, which feels itself to be so limited, to comprehend the fact that there is a power that makes things directly out of itself by simply becoming the thing that it makes, and that it does this by self-knowing. We will not demonstrate until we see at least some of this, the greatest truth about life.

We should realize that we are dealing with a principle that is scientifically correct. It will never fail us at any time. It is eternally present. We can approach the infinite mind with a depth of thought and understanding, knowing that it will respond and knowing that we are dealing with reality.

Jesus, who saw this very clearly, laid down the whole law of life in a few simple words: "It is done unto you as you believe." We do not have to do it; it is done unto us. It is done by a power that is all. If we believed that a mountain will be moved, it would be done unto us. But unless we do believe, there is no impulse for the creative power and we will not receive. Life externalizes at the level of our thought.

ACTION AND REACTION

• • •

There is something that throws back to us every thought that we think. "Vengeance is mine; I will repay, says the Lord" is a statement of eternal truth and correspondences against which nothing can stand. Whatever we set in motion in mind will be returned to us, even as we have conceived within ourselves and brought forth into manifestation.

If we wish to transcend old thoughts, we must rise above them and think higher things. We are dealing with the law of cause and effect, and it is absolute. It receives the slightest, as well as the greatest, thought, and at once begins to act on it. Even when we know this, we are sometimes surprised at the rapidity with which it works.

If we have been misusing this law, we need not fail. All that we have to do is turn from the old way and begin in the new. We will soon work up out of the old law and into the new that is being established for us. When we desire only the good, the evil slips from us and returns no more.

Arriving at a High Consciousness

* * *

The best way to arrive at the highest consciousness is to have great faith in the willingness and the ability of life to do everything for us by working through us. We must believe in the inherent goodness and all-powerfulness of the Spirit of truth.

Every path leads us back to the one point, and we must learn to realize the near presence, the great reality. There, through the door of our own thought, we enter into the universal consciousness, into a complete realization of life and truth, of love and beauty. As we sit in the silence of our own soul and listen, it will be the greatest thing that we will ever do. In that completeness, we are lost, and yet we are found. This is what is meant that we must lose our life in order to find it. We are lost to the human and found in the divine. We realize that we are one with cause.

OUTER SUGGESTIONS

❋   ❋   ❋

Most people are controlled by outer suggestions and not inner realizations. Ordinarily, people think only what they see others do and hear only what others say. We must all learn to control the inner life so that outside things do not make an impression on our mentalities. Since we are thinking beings and cannot help but think, we cannot avoid making things happen to us. We need to control our thought processes so that our thinking will not depart from the realization of that which is perfect.

Humankind is governed by a mind that casts back to us every thought we think. We cannot escape from this and need not try; it would be useless. The laws of mind are simple and easy to understand. The trouble with us is that we lay down great obstructions and then try to overcome them. Stop trying. Stop struggling. Begin to be calm, to trust in the higher laws of life. Even though you do not see them, they are still there.

Have you ever seen the law that causes a plant to grow? Of course you haven't, and yet you believe in this hidden law of growth. Why do you believe? Simply because every year out of the seed time comes a harvest. Will you not have as great a faith in the higher laws of being? To those who have dared to believe has come as definite an answer as that which has come to those who believed in receiving a harvest from the planted seed. The law *is*, and if we see results, we must use it. We must provide the mental receptivity that will prepare us to accept the gift when the Spirit makes it. This receiving is a mental process, a process in which we lose all sense of limitation.

If you wish to demonstrate prosperity, begin to think and talk about it and to see it everywhere. Do nothing that contradicts this thought, either mentally or physically. The world is full of good. Take it, and forget all else. Rise above depression, and be glad that you are saved from adversity. The human mind needs to be cleansed from the morbid thoughts that bind it through false beliefs.

No living soul can demonstrate two things at the same time, not if one contradicts the other. There is no way except to let go of all that you do not wish to come into your experience and, in mind, take all that you do wish.

See, hear, talk about, and read only what you wish for, and never again let a negative thought come into your mind.

God knows only good, and when we are in line with good, God knows us. When we are out of harmony with good, we say, "God has forgotten us." On one hand, we have an infinite intelligence that has brought us up to where we are today. Having done all that it can for us, it now lets us alone to discover our own nature. On the other hand, we have the infinite law, which is an activity of God. We can use it for what we will only as long as we use it for the good of all.

The law says that as we sow, so must we reap. Spirit has brought us to where we can understand life, and we must do as we choose. If we are in harmony with the great forward movement of the Spirit, there is nothing that can hinder our advancement. If we oppose it, somewhere along our pathway it will crush us. As with individuals, so with nations. As long as they work with a right spirit, they prosper; when they begin to fail in the use of this law, they begin to fall. Those who understand this will take the position of one who wishes to work in union with the power of good, and to such individuals will come all the power that they can conceive of and believe in. Their word becomes in expression as the very word of God, and they must realize it to be all powerful.

The ones who are truly united with good will wish to express only the truth for all, and in doing so, they are working along the lines of the unfoldment of the Spirit. Though they may seem to fail from the ordinary standpoint, their success is assured because they are at one with the only ultimate power before which, in time, all else must fall.

THE USE OF THE GREATER CONSCIOUSNESS

＊　　＊　　＊

In practice, the emancipated soul must always realize that it is in union with the Spirit. What the Spirit does, the emancipated soul can do in its own life. What God is, the emancipated soul can become. The soul's word must be spoken with absolute authority. It must *know*. There should be no uncertainty. The word is the only power; everything must come from it and nothing can stand against it. It is the great weapon that the emancipated soul is to use against all evil and for all good. It is its shield against all adversity and its sure defense against all seeming limitation.

The secret place of the Most High is in the soul, where God dwells in eternal peace and infinite calm. Here, the soul walks the waters of life undisturbed by the waves and the storm. Divine companionship belongs to the emancipated soul for all eternity. Peace that transcends all human confusion comes, and the emancipated soul realizes that it is, indeed, honored of the Spirit. The soul's word is flung out and will work, and nothing can hinder it. The sense of sureness is complete. Heaven and earth may pass away, but the word goes on and on accomplishing that thing for which it was sent, and all power is given to it on earth and in heaven. If the soul speaks to the sick and they receive, they will be healed. If it says the word of prosperity, it will manifest, and nothing can hinder it. The world will abound with good, and the soul's cup runs over with life.

What greater realization of life than to know that God is with us! From this realization comes peace, a peace that the world little understands and a calm that is as deep as the infinite sea of love in which each soul realizes itself to be immersed. Peace brings poise, and the union of these two gives birth to power.

We cannot hope to arrive if we believe in two powers. Only as we rise to the realization of the one in and through everything can we attain. When we speak the word, there must be no confusion, but only that calm reliance that knows that "beside me there is none other." Realize that Spirit is all causation, that all things are made out of it by the operation of the word through it, and that you can speak the word that is one with the Spirit. Then, there will be no more confusion. As parents have inherent life in themselves, so have they given to their children to have inherent life within them. "Speak the word only and it shall be done." "The word is in your own mouth that you should know it and do it." "Stranger on earth, your home is heaven; pilgrim, you are the guest of God."

THE GREATER CONSCIOUSNESS

*　*　*

Humankind is surrounded by a great universal thought power that always returns to us exactly as we think. This mind is so plastic, so receptive, that it takes the slightest impression and molds it into conditions. There are two things that our thought affects: our body, and our environment. At all times, we are given absolute control over these two things, and we cannot hope to escape from the effect of our thought on them.

At first, being ignorant of this fact, we bind ourselves by a misuse of the laws. But as we begin to see that we ourselves are responsible for all that comes to us on the path of life, we begin to control our thought, which in turn acts on the universal substance to create for us a new world.

The great soul is learning more and more to fling into mind a divine idea of itself and to see itself perfect and whole.

If we have a divine thought, we will get a divine thing; if we have a human thought, we will get a human thing. We will receive whatever our innermost thought embodies. The Bible twice repeats these words: "To the pure, God will show God's self pure, and to the forward, God will show God's self forward." It is done unto us as we believe.

We often wonder why we are not making better demonstrations. We look around and observe that some people are getting wonderful results. They are speaking their word and people are being healed. We see others struggle with the word and nothing seems to happen. When we look into this, we find the answer to be simple. All is mind, and we are mental. We are in mind and can only get from it what we first think into it. We must not only think, but we must know. We have to provide within ourselves a mental and spiritual likeness for the thing desired.

The reason so many fail, then, must be because they have not mentally believed to the exclusion of all that would deny the thing in which they believe. The reason why others succeed must be because they have absolutely believed and allowed real power to flow through and out into expression. They must have a real concept of life. Hold an object in front of a mirror and it will image in the mirror the exact size of the object. Hold a thought in mind and it will reflect in matter the exact likeness of the thought. When we take this image that we hold before a mirror and change it ever so slightly, there will be a corresponding change in the reflection. It is exactly the same in the mental world. Whatever is imagined is brought forth from mind into manifestation.

We must not deny that which we affirm. We must reason only from the cause that is spiritual and mental, and weed out all thought that would deny its power in our lives. There seems to be something in the collective unconscious that says humankind is poor, humankind is limited, there is a lack of opportunity, times are tough, prices are high, and nobody wants what I have to offer. No person succeeds who speaks these ideas. When we express ourselves in this way, we are using a destructive power. All such thoughts must go, and we must realize that we are each an active center in the only power there is.

We must get the perfect vision, the perfect conception. We must enlarge our thought until it realizes all good, and then we must swing right out and use this almighty power for definite purposes. On a daily basis, we should feel a deeper union with life, a greater sense of that indwelling God, the God of the everywhere within us. When we speak into this mind, we sow the seed of thought in the absolute and may relax. We do not have to make haste, because it is done to us as we believe. "In that day that they shall call upon me, I will answer."

People might ask, "What is the best method for demonstration?" The only answer to that question is, "The word is the only possible method of demonstrating anything—the word truly felt and embodied in thought." Then the word becomes flesh and dwells among us, and we behold and experience it. We will ask for no other way when we understand this.

The person who does not understand these laws will likely say that this is presumptuous, that it is even sacrilegious, but this comes only from a lack of understanding that all is governed by law and that all law is impersonal and universal. We have just as much right to use spiritual law as to use physical laws. Strictly speaking, there is no such a thing as a physical law, because all things are spiritual and all law is a law of the activity of the Spirit. The greatest use of these laws will always come to that one who is the most deeply spiritual, because this person comes the nearest to using law as God uses it.

To the great soul there must come a very close relationship with the invisible God. This relationship cannot be expressed in words, but only in inner feeling that transcends the power of words to express. God must become the great reality, not simply as the principle of life, but more as the great mind that knows and at all times understands and responds. To say that God does not understand our desires would be to rob the divine mind of all consciousness and place God lower in the scale of being than we ourselves are. On the other hand, we must be careful not to believe that God thinks evil and understands that which is not perfect, because then we would have an imperfect Spirit for the first cause.

We should learn to think more of things in the absolute, that is, to think of things as not limited by conditions. Realizing at all times that the Spirit makes things out of itself and needs no beginning except its own self-recognition, we must perceive our relation to this great power as one of absolute correspondence. What we think into it, it takes up and does for us as we think.

It should not be an effort to think. We should do so with ease, not strain. The law has to return to us. We have no responsibility except to provide the proper channel. It can return only in the exact way that we think. If we think struggle is our reality, we will gain our demonstration, but struggle will have to be the result.

There is a law of reflection between mind and the one who thinks. It is not only what we think, but also *how* we think that "shall be done unto us."

If we absolutely believe that we can do a certain thing,

the way will always be opened for us to do it. If we believe that time will have to elapse, we then make that a law, and time will have to elapse. If, though, you believe that mind knows how and never makes mistakes, but lets it be done unto us, then it will be done.

Confusion brings more confusion; peace begets more peace. The Spirit does not hurry or worry or try to make anything happen. The only reason we worry and fret is because we think there is some other power that could bring confusion. But this is not the case. There is only *one*, and we are always using that one according to our belief. This is our divine birthright. Nothing hinders but ourselves.

Remember, since all is mind, you cannot demonstrate beyond your ability to mentally comprehend, that is, beyond your ability to know about a certain thing. For instance, suppose you wish to heal someone who is sick. Your ability to do this will depend entirely on your ability to mentally see perfection, coupled with the realization that your word destroys everything unlike itself. If you try to see perfection for only a few minutes, it will never heal. Your thought goes on at all times, and in the moments when you least realize it, conditions are being molded for you. It is not enough to declare consciously for the truth. The truth must be lived, otherwise no good results will be coming.

THE PERFECT UNIVERSE

* * *

The one who desires to heal must stop seeing, reading about, discussing or listening to conversations about sickness. There is no other way under the sun except to let go of that which we do not desire and take that which we wish to have. We deceive ourselves too much into thinking that we can do two ways at once. We may trick ourselves, and possibly other people, but the law remains the same. It is a law of mental correspondences and nothing else.

We cannot go beyond our ability to realize the truth. Water rises only to its own level. In the people for whom we pray, as well as in ourselves and our environment, we will reflect what we are, not at our best in the few moments of meditation, but in the long run of ordinary life and thought.

To acquire a larger consciousness is no easy task. All belief that contradicts the perfect whole must be dropped from our thought, and we must come to realize that we are now living in a perfect universe, peopled with perfect spiritual beings, all of whom are complete within themselves. We must see that we are one in the great Spirit, and then we will not separate or divide, but unite and add to, until in time we find that we are living in an entirely different world from that in which we once thought we were living. This will meet with much opposition from unenlightened souls we come in contact with in the world. But what of that? Remember, the great person is the one who can keep calm in the crowd and maintain a deep, divine reliance on principle. This is the only way to help or to save the world. In time, all people will come to the same understanding. You are lifting up the standard of life, and those who are ready will follow. You have no responsibility to save the world except by exemplifying the truth. The world must save itself.

Everyone is alike. There is no difference between one person and another. Come to see everyone as a divine idea. Stop all negative thought. Think only about what you want and never about what you do not want, because that would cause a false creation. Too much cannot be said about the fact that we are dealing with only one power, making and unmaking for all people through the creative power of their own thought. If there is something in your life that you do not want there, stop fighting it—forget it!

ABOUT STRUGGLE—KARMA

* * *

There is too much struggle seeping into spiritual thought. Often, we hear some student of truth say, "I have a big fight ahead." This is foolish talk! The realm of heaven comes not from without, but from within, always. Stop all struggle, and wait upon the sure principle that creates whatever it wills because there is nothing to oppose it. As long as we think that opposition exists, we are blocking the way for the clearer vision. Those who take up the sword must perish by it, not because God is a jealous God, but because that is the way the law must work.

Cause and effect must apply everywhere. Do not fuss about your karma. Too often, people say, "It is my karma." This may be true, but how many people know what they mean when they use the word *karma*? Karma is nothing but your false thinking. The only way to escape it and bring in the higher law is to think the truth. When the greater comes in, the lesser leaves because there is no longer anything to give life to it. The past is gone when we learn to forgive and forget.

This erases from mind all that is held against us, and even our sins "are remembered no more against us forever." Fate is in our own hands. When we will rise to that pure atmosphere where we see things in their completeness and know that an all-wise power is behind it all, we will see that the infinite mind could wish for us only that which expresses itself in limitless terms. The whole trouble has been that we reason as human beings and not as gods. "I say you are gods, and every one of you children of the Most High."

The great law of life is thinking and becoming, and when we think from the lofty heights of the Spirit, we will become great, and not until then. Do not try to convince anyone of the truth. That only brings confusion. Truth *is*, just as much as God *is*, and the whole world is gradually coming into the realization of it. Keep the truth within your own soul. Lift your own self above the confusion of life, and then people will believe. All your thought is to be created in the realization of the one becoming the many, without struggle, without fear, stripped of all that denies the truth.

We limit ourselves too much. Our thoughts are too small. The human race rises in the morning, plods off to the day's work, plods home at night, sore and tired, eats and sleeps, works and dies. As has been said of humankind, "People work hard to get money to buy food to get strength to work hard to get money to buy food to get strength to work hard to get money..." This was never the intention. It is a curse imposed on those who believe in two powers, one of good and one of evil. To us, there has come a greater vision, and to those who believe and act as though it were true, it is proving itself.

We must turn from all human thought and experience. We are not downtrodden, depraved, and miserable sinners, born in sin and conceived in iniquity and shame, some to go to heaven and some to hell, and all to the eternal glory of God. This is a lie; it always was and always will be. But as long as we believe in a lie, it seems to be true.

Humankind is born of the Spirit of God. It is pure, holy, perfect, complete, and undefiled. All people are at one with the eternal principle of being. Many people are discovering this, and millions are daily proving it for themselves.

Somewhere down the path of human experience, we

will all wake up to the realization that we ourselves are heaven or hell.

We live in Spirit, awaiting the touch of thought that believes. All people look; a few see.

Part 2

Practice

❊   ❊   ❊

INTRODUCTORY

* * *

Those of us who wish to study spiritual philosophy must first, last, and always realize that we ourselves are each a center of the divine activity. We must know that whatever God is in the universal, we are in the world in which we live. We must know that all things are made out of Spirit, which is first cause; nothing comes before Spirit. Operating on and out of itself, it makes what it will out of its own perfect desire. We must think of the Spirit as the creator of our lives, eternally bound to us, eternally binding us to it.

We must know that not only can the Spirit manifest through us, but that it wishes to do so. "Spirit seeks such to worship." We who understand the truth know that as long as God exists, we will exist, that we could no more become non-existent than God could. Walking, talking, moving in God, we must not only see the divine being as the great unknown cause, but we must go a step further and see God as the self-knowing, understanding power of infinite intelligence thinking through our thoughts and willing into our lives all power and all good. More than this, God must become within our own souls the greater self, the inner life, the inner light that is to light our paths with sure steps to the attainment of greater ideals. God is to become the great friend of our lives, understanding us and helping us at all times to understand all things.

We do not need more books, more teachers, more preachers, creeds, or candlesticks. The old methods must vanish into their native nothingness as the great realization that God is all in our lives dawns on our awakened thoughts.

We must know that neither height nor depth nor any other thing can come between the soul and its perfect creator. We have listened to other people for too long. Now, our own souls will speak in a language that is unmistakable. Now, we ourselves will become masters of all life and interpreters of all mysteries. Now, my creator and I are one.

As the word of God goes forth and sets in motion all law, so must we realize that because we are one with the word, our own thought has the power of expression. The one who wishes to heal must come to see all evil as impersonal, fastening it to no one, but realizing that it is simply false thought. Healers know that the word they speak will destroy this false impression, and that by erasing it, it will vanish.

There should be absolutely no sense of responsibility beyond speaking the word in positive faith and simply knowing. Struggle belongs to the old order; in the new, peace takes the place of confusion, faith answers the cry of doubt and fear, and the word is supreme.

Our word is law and cannot be set aside by the false thought of the world. Every time we state a truth, we must know that the truth destroys all that is unlike itself and frees the thought of the one whom we wish to help and heal.

This word must become the new law that frees. People are sick because they think sickness, and they will be healed only when they turn from this kind of thought and begin to think in terms of health.

THE SAME POWER USED IN TWO WAYS

*   *   *

There is only one power, but we use it in two ways: to destroy, and to save. A blessing and a curse are one in the same thing. Both are the power of mind used either affirmatively or negatively. They are the word used in fear and doubt, or in faith and assurance.

You do not have to understand philosophy or be learned in the books of the human race. All these things may be good in their place, but to one who understands the greater laws of life, they are as simple babblings. We no longer ask if there is a God. We do not analyze, dissect, affirm, or deny. We know.

We trust our own word, because we "know in whom we have believed." The sooner we who strive to attain realize that truth is revealed through our own souls and not those of another, the sooner we will attain.

We must then become immune from the collective belief in a hypnotic power that sets itself up as an authority. There is no authority other than your own soul, just as "there is no law but that your soul has set." Be free, and leave authorities to smaller minds and to those who need a leader because of their self-confessed weakness. Dare to "stand amidst the eternal way" and proclaim your own *at-one-ment* with all the power that there is, was, or ever will be.

Most of the human race is hypnotized, thinking whatever it is told to think. We get our concepts from our physical environment. We see sin, sickness, death, misery, unhappiness, and calamity, and we attribute these concepts to the creative, impersonal mind. Thus, we make a law for ourselves that will produce what we believe in. Do we really know what law means? It means that which will exact the utmost molecule from our thought.

Like produces like, attracts like, and creates like. If we could take a photograph of our thoughts and our conditions, we would see no difference between the two, because they are actually the inside and the outside of the same thing.

To obtain the results we seek, we cannot pray for fifteen minutes and then spend the rest of our day denying the thing for which we have prayed and praying for the thing that we have denied. When we do this, we send out the word, which sets the power in motion, and then we think the opposite thing, which neutralizes the first word, and the result is zero.

We cannot demonstrate one iota beyond our mental ability to conceive and steadfastly embody. Infinite, receptive, and quick as creative power is, it can only become to us what we first think into it. God can only do for us what God can do through us.

Dare to say, "Behold, I am the one. Great people have come and gone, and behold, a greater now stands here where I stand, and I am that one." The world might laugh at or ridicule you. Christians may hold up their hands in horror because you blaspheme. The unchristian world will smile knowingly. Neither one nor the other will understand, but the understanding of either counts for nothing. You are now free, and your freedom will save the world from itself.

The great soul finds within itself the divine companionship that it needs. It finds within itself the "peace which passes all understanding" and the power to do all things. *All power!* It speaks, its word is law, and it is done unto it by all the power there is. Its word knows itself to be the law of life to all for whom it is spoken and who receive it.

HEALING THE SICK

* * *

We will be called on to heal all manner of disease, to comfort the sorrowful, and to bring peace to the distressed. First, though, we must heal ourselves.

When we are healing others, we are also healing ourselves. A healer's work takes place within. This idea of "sending out thought" or "holding thought" is a mistake. Things come into being not only by "taking thought," but by knowing that the word is infinite. This word is in your own mouth, and there alone can it be spoken. Here, your responsibility begins, and here it ends, in your own mouth.

You must feel no responsibility for the recovery of the person for whom you pray, because it brings confusion and disorder if you are always wondering whether it is working. If you have the sure faith and the recipient is receptive, it must work. You are dealing with the same power that said, "Let there be light" and there was light.

If the people for whom you are praying are suffering from a belief that they are dying of some awful disease, you must know that when you speak the word, it will destroy this false belief and set them free. There must be no doubt about the power in the word that you speak. It should be said in perfect calm, in peace, and with absolute faith that it works. This word then establishes the law of life onto the patient. It casts out all fear. It destroys all false sense of a material life and realizes that all is an expression of a perfect God, leaving nothing that can sin, be sick, suffer, or die. When you are as sure of this as you are that you breathe, when you truly know within yourself, your patients will be healed, provided they also believe. If they do not believe, it is not your fault, and you will have done for them all that can be done.

DENIALS

* * *

Some people teach the use of denials. This must be settled by all people for themselves. Here and at all times, we must settle every question from within and not from without. No living soul can say how another should or should not work. Beware of the danger of a self-appointed authority. This danger is as apt to come into the new thought as it was in the old. No one is your authority on anything.

When we look into the philosophy of denials, we find that many people teach and practice them, and we do not wish in any way to criticize them. Their reasoning is this: All disease is an image of thought held in mind until it appears in the body. It is true that without the ability to think, people could not be sick. If one thinks a sick thought, it will make one sick; when one changes one's thought and thinks health, one is healed. Some feel that since sickness is a negative thought, it must be counter-acted by a positive thought, and the best way is to deny the sickness and affirm the positive thought. For instance, "There is no matter, so nothing can be the matter. This person has no material stomach. This person is spiritual, not material. This person's lungs are not made of matter; they are spiritual ideas. I deny that any person can be sick or suffer or die." All this is accurate. All people are spiritual ideas and so must be perfect in their real nature. The question is whether this is the better way to pray.

When we look into the creative way of Spirit, we find it impossible for denial to enter, because the Spirit recognizes no opposite to its own nature. It knows that "I am, and beside me there is no other." The Spirit does not deny anything; it simply affirms itself to be that which it desires to be. Recognizing no opposite to itself, it finds no need for denial. Indeed, this thought need not enter the mind. When we work with the Spirit, we need not deny, but rather state the affirmative attitude of mind, realizing that we are dealing with the only power that exists.

There is a subtle danger in using denials. We may deny to such an extent that we erect a barrier or build a mountain that we will need to overcome later. Once we realize that God makes things out of itself simply by speaking, we will never again use denials when praying. The only thing that needs changing is the false thought.

By affirming that our word destroys everything except itself, we will embody all that a denial could. In those systems that teach denials, we find that the more enlightened students are gradually using the affirmative method. The Spirit never denies. It simply knows that *I am*.

THE USE OF AFFIRMATIVE PRAYER

* * *

The affirmation is the great weapon of the healer. It is in alignment with the way of the original, creative Spirit and is the true use of the word of all power. We only need to say that our word is the law, calmly state what we want to be done, and then say or do nothing that contradicts it. There is a power that operates on what we say. It is done unto us, and we need to have no fear about the results.

If I am praying for a patient, I only need to go to work within myself to realize that this person is now a perfect being, made in the image of God. I must know that I am destroying all imperfection. When I know within myself that I am speaking the truth and that the patient is perfect, the healing is done as far as I am concerned.

If the patient receives, there is a healing. I am not responsible for the receptivity of the patient. When you know that there is a power that corresponds to your own mental attitude, you will see that the way you believe is what makes things happen the way they do. Always believe in what you are doing. Never see the negative side of life. Never talk about it or listen to talk of other people, and never think about or see imperfection. When you do this, you will have no trouble in making demonstrations.

THE HIGHEST ATTITUDE OF MIND

* * *

The highest attitude of mind from which all else springs is one of perfect calm and absolute trust in the Spirit. Those who most completely demonstrate the supremacy of spiritual thought over material resistance are the ones who look into the future with perfect confidence, rest in the present with perfect ease of mind, and never look backward. They have learned to be still in their own souls and wait upon the Spirit.

"Be still, and know that I am God."

NON-RESISTANCE

* * *

"Resist not evil, and it will flee from you." This is one of the great laws of our existence. When we resist, we make a mental image of the thing we are fighting, which tends to create it for us. When we look only at what we want and not at what we do not want, we will no longer resist anything.

"Suffer it to be so now." You do not need to change the world. Leave it alone. Everyone is doing the best they can. No one needs to be saved but ourselves, and the sooner we realize this, the sooner we will succeed. Get over that "holier than thou" attitude. It is an illusion that many people suffer from, especially in the religious world. The world is all right. It is not going to hell; it is on the way to heaven. It is getting good so quickly that, in the process, many things are being overturned and seem confused. A great change is taking place. On the surface, the results are as yet a little mixed, but underneath, the power is at work destroying everything unlike itself. In time, we will all come to see this. What a load of responsibility we assume that we were never meant to carry!

In the divine plan, no mistakes are made. If God could have done it in a better way, it would have been done differently. No soul is ever lost, because everyone "lives and moves and has their being in God" and "God is not a God of the dead, but of the living, for in God's sight, all are alive." We have believed in the negative for too long simply because we have allowed ourselves to become hypnotized by a few strong-minded people, by those who have imposed a mass of false philosophy on the rest of us.

Be Alive

* * *

There is no place in the new order for "dead weight." True spiritual philosophers are alive to everything that is useful. Taking our places in the events of the human history, we take part in all its work and all its play. Pessimism must be thrown on the scrap heap. There is no place among the living for the dead. "Let the dead bury their dead." "Follow me." Do not hesitate to enter into the game of life, but do so with a zest and enthusiasm that overflows with life. Fill yourself with the radiance of a life running over with power and usefulness. Then, the world will see your light.

Above all others, students of spiritual philosophy should enter into the business world, into educational vocations, into politics, into every walk of life, and in those positions prove that they are not children of humanity, but children of God.

Be Happy

* * *

How can we help the world see the right way unless we overflow with joy ourselves? The world is full of sad faces. We see them everywhere, in those resigned looks that seem to say, "One rejection more or less makes no difference. I am already so sad that nothing matters. I can bear it." This was all right when we thought everything was all wrong, but now we know that "all's well with the world." We must get over this depression that robs us of the power of attraction of the good things of life and enter in.

Those who are always glad will surround themselves with people who are happy, and life will be a continual enjoyment. This robs no one. It does not make a race of irresponsible people; it makes a world of joy, a world that is good to live in.

No one wants to associate with the dead. People are looking for a more abundant expression of life, not for depression and fault-finding. Find fault with no one, and, more than this, find no fault with yourself. Get over the thought of condemning people and things. People and things are all right; let them alone and enjoy life. Your very atmosphere will cheer and uplift the people who contact you, and a new life will enter into them. Overflow!

LIVE IN THE PRESENT

* * *

Life is for us *today*. There will be no change for tomorrow unless we change today. Right now, we are setting in motion the power of tomorrow. Today is God's day, and we must extract from it the life we want to live. Tomorrow, the divine course of events will take care of itself. The soul that learns to live in the gladness of today will never weary of life, but will find that it is living in an eternal here and now. Now, all good is yours. Now, all life, truth, and love are yours. Now, you have entered in, and the good things of life are yours today.

Let your soul sing today, and the song that comes tomorrow will be all the sweeter. It will ring out over the vistas of time with an unmistakable clearness, "Here is a soul that knows itself and has found life within itself, one who has met God today!" No more waiting, no more longing, no more weary roads to travel. You have arrived. The goal is won, and peace has come at last. Today!

See the Good in All Things

* * *

Learn to see God in everything—in all people and through all events. The ordinary person sees only material substance. The awakened soul, though, sees the divine mind at work in all things, molding out into expression what it feels itself to be of life, of color, of form, and of beauty. There are some pessimistic people who claim that what we see is false and that the so-called material universe is an unreality. They are wrong! What we see is the body of God, full, free, complete, and whole.

One never sees the idea behind a thing; a thing is seen only as matter, matter, matter. What we can see is God's thought of ourselves expressing in an infinite variety of forms. What do we see when we look at the human form, the crowning glory of God's perfect creation? Matter, matter, matter? Flesh, blood, and bones? It is true that these may be passing into expression, but what of the idea, what of the reality of the body?

Our bodies are as real as God is real. They would not be if they were illusions. The touch of the flesh should send a thrill through the whole body, raising its vibration to a higher pitch, to a finer form. The body is not a "mass of pollution." It is the temple of the living God and should be thought of as such. We have condemned it for too long, and now we must free it by reversing the process. Of all things on earth, the human body is the most beautiful, the most wonderful, and the most godlike.

"If you do not love your neighbor, whom you have seen, how can you love God, whom you have not seen?" Human magnetism is not hypnotism. It is the divinity of humankind in expression, and when we learn to convert human passion into divine love, to transmute the lower into the higher, we will have a power of attraction against which nothing can stand.

"Those who have ears to hear, let them hear."

When we observe a beautiful sunset, we should see the wonderful thought of God, the radiance of God's presence. In the strength of the hills, we should see the strength of the Spirit, and seeing all things as spiritual ideas, we should learn to love them, because God has made them and given them to us to use. The soul who can rush up to a tree in ecstasy and embrace it realizes more of God than all the priests who have ever lived. The one who can smell the ocean breeze with delight feels the presence of the divine presence more keenly than the one who kneels in despair before an awful God of justice.

Learn, then, how to appreciate nature and nature's God. Spend time in the outdoors. Look up at the stars. Let them be your companions. Tread the pathless ways of the trees and the giant forests, and see God in everything that you look on, the God of the everywhere.

Be Expectant

* * *

Expect the best to happen. Don't sit around waiting for trouble. Have absolutely nothing to do with it. It is no part of the divine plan. It is an illusion of the material senses.

We who have learned to trust will not be surprised, even when we find things coming from the most unexpected sources. All things are ours to use and then let go of. What more can we ask? We want nothing that we have to keep. Things are to use, not to hold.

Expect that everything is coming your way. Be content and cheerful if you wish to attract from the store of the infinite. Open up your whole consciousness to the greater possibilities of life. Line up with the big things.

When you speak the word, expect it to happen. Know that it must be as you say. This will not be fooling yourself. It will simply be using the law as it is meant to be used.

EXPANDING OUR THOUGHT

※　　※　　※

All things come to us through the use of our thought. If we have a small concept of life, we will always be doing small things. First is the word, but the word carries us no further than our consciousness behind it. Unless we are constantly expanding our thought, we are not growing. Growth is the law of life, and it is necessary. We cannot stand still. If we want to do a new thing, we must get a new thought. Then we will have the power of attraction that has the possibility of drawing to us the circumstances that will make for the fulfillment of our desires.

Get over the old idea of limitation. Overcome all precedents, and set yourself in the new order of things. If you want to build a skyscraper, you will never do it unless you get over the idea that the most you can hope for in life is to sell peanuts. Let the people who think in the terms of peanuts sell peanuts for a living. Get out of the rut. God has created you for a glorious future. Dare to fling into mind the greater assurances about yourself.

The Power of Affirmative Prayer

* * *

Affirmative prayer has as much power as we put into the word that we speak when we are praying. This does not mean using willpower or force from the material standpoint. It simply means knowing that what we say will be done unto us by a power that can do anything it is given to do. We must know that our word breaks down every material law and sets the recipient of the prayer free to express God. We must know that the word would endure even though everything else should fail. "Heaven and earth will pass away, but my word will accomplish." In calm confidence and perfect faith, speak and wait on the perfect law. Get that mental attitude that never wavers. Be sure, and it will be done.

Repeating the Affirmative Prayer

*   *   *

One affirmative prayer would heal anything if it were not for the fact that we are constantly receiving false suggestions from the outer world. As it now stands, we should pray until we get results, always expecting that results will happen at once. Every affirmative prayer should be complete. At the close, we should always realize that it is done.

The word spoken from the mind that knows is immediately taken up by the mind in which we live, and this mind begins to create around the word, which is the seed, the thing thought of. We must speak that word with authority. There can be no wondering if it is going to work. When we plant a seed in the ground and then water and care for it, we never doubt that a plant will spring into being. So it is with the word. It is acted on by a power that we do not see, but there is no doubt that the power is there, since all who go about it get results.

As Thomas Edison said of electricity, "It is; use it." So we say of mind, "It is; use it." Always remember that our every thought is the way that we are praying, because it is the way that we are thinking.

Impersonal Healing

* * *

The very presence of one who understands the truth will have a great power of healing. The reason is that we are all in mind, and we have our thought with us at all times. Since all manifestation is the result of mind in action, and since we are thinking beings always causing mind to act, the very presence of our thought will have some power to act on whatever we are thinking about.

We are dealing with a power that, in itself, is limitless. We limit it, and so it cannot become to us the bigger thing. Of itself, the power is the same that made the worlds, and it cannot realize any sense of limitation. "They could not enter in because of their unbelief and because they limited the holy one of Israel."

Stop limiting things. Things are as big as we make them, no more, no less. There is room at the top. Get on top of everything and dare to dominate the earth. All things are given us to use, so make use of them. Everything is limitless, and we must see that when we fail, the fault is not in the law but in ourselves. Not with God, but with us. Dare! Think of the bigness of things in the universe. Think of the number of grains of sand, the profusion of all life, and never again limit anything. All is yours to use. Jesus would never have become the Christ unless he had the courage to say, "Behold, I am it." You will never attain until in some degree you are able to say the same thing of yourself.

We must learn to reach out and take what is meant for us, which is the greater life, the all good. People say, "Yes, but how do you do it?" Simply know that God makes things out of itself by speaking the word, and that in our own lives we can do the same.

All of us can think and all of us can speak, at least mentally. This is all that we need to begin. The word is at the center of all creation and is first cause, the starting point of all that we see. The word is in our own mouths, and all that we have to do is to speak it. The trouble is that we speak the word with one breath and deny its power by seeing something that contradicts it with the next breath. If the word is the way that God creates, it is the right way. If it works for God, it will work for us.

So far, our word is more or less imperfect, but more and more it will become perfect. Then, the outer condition will be brought up to the inner word. All words have as much power as we put into them when we speak. "The word is already in our own mouths." That word is all that we will ever need to bring happiness, health, and success to our lives.

Do you wish to live in a perfect world peopled with friends who love you, surrounded by all that is beautiful and pleasing? Do you wish to have the good things of life? There is only one way, and that way is as sure as that the sun shines. Forget all else and think only about what you want. Control all thought that denies the truth, and just like the fog disappears before the sun, so will adversity melt before the shining radiance of your own exalted thought.

In the Bible, the prodigal remained a prodigal only as long as he chose to do so. When the thought came to him to return, he was greeted by his father with outstretched hands. When we turn to the world that is perfect, there will be something that will turn with us, and we will behold the new heaven and the new earth. We will become free, not in some far-off place beyond the clouds, but here and now.

We must do away with all that hinders true growth,

all the little thoughts that hold us back from becoming. Human strife comes from the thought that there is not enough to go around. Forget it. We cannot even use everything that we can see, and what we cannot see is infinite. You will rob no one by becoming prosperous. The laws that underlie this state of being are simple to understand and easy to attain for the one who is willing to let go of the negative state of being.

Prosperity

* * *

Here are a few simple rules for prosperity that are as sure of working as water is sure to be wet. First, nothing happens by chance. Everything is law and all is order. We create our own laws every time we think. There is a power around us—call it what you will—that knows and that understands all things. This power works like the soil. It receives the seed of our thought and at once begins to operate on it. It will receive, create, and return to us whatever we think into it.

This means that prayer practitioners should be very careful how they are thinking at all times. We are praying for our patients in an impersonal way at all times, not only when we are alone in moments of deep silence.

When we take patients into our thought for affirmative prayer, we send a constant stream of consciousness flowing out to them during all the time that they are in our care. We should be very careful of our thoughts as we realize the deep truths of mental action and reaction.

What Is the Spiritual Mind?

*   *   *

What is true spirituality? Many people have asked this, and as many have answered it. To the thinking person who has come to realize that all is love yet, at the same time, all is governed by law, there must be a different answer to this question than the one we ordinarily hear.

The average religious person thinks that spirituality must manifest in some unnatural way, such as by giving up personal pleasure or becoming resigned to whatever happens or by giving up most of what life holds here so that in some far-off future perhaps we may attain. This was not the case with Jesus. We have more accounts of his being at feasts and weddings and similar gatherings than at other places. His first miracle was performed at a wedding feast, where he turned water into wine for the pleasure of the guests of the house. Maybe we have made a mistake about what true spirituality means.

Other people think we must live some kind of exclusive life in order to obtain. Perhaps this is true for weak people, but what of the world? What of the busy street? Is it not to be saved also? Jesus spent time with the common people as well as with the rich. It is certain that he also spent much time alone with the Spirit.

What is the Spirit, anyway? We answer, "Why, of course, it is God." Where is the Spirit? It is present at all times and in all places. True spirituality simply means coming to realize the presence of this Spirit. It means relying on it more than anything else. Those who are the most spiritual are simply the ones who rely the most. That is all. No matter where they are, they must rely, they must trust, and they must believe. We do not have to give up anything but negative thought, and then we act. We do not want to do anything that contradicts the forward march of the Spirit, so all that we think and do must be in line with that which is right.

But who says what is right and what is not? Remember this forever: Only your own soul says what is right and what is wrong. "To your own self be true, and it shall follow as the night the day, you can not then be false to anyone." Look to no one for guidance. This is the "blind leading the blind." Spirit has put the truth into your own soul. Look for it there and there alone.

Praise and blame sound alike to one who knows the truth. From the human standpoint at least, a person cannot help being amused at the way in which the world judges true spirituality. My idea of true spirituality is all people living perfectly normal lives, entering into and enjoying everything in life that is clean and good. We should place ourselves absolutely under the divine guidance. Otherwise, we will seem just like everyone else, neither better nor worse.

We should get over unnatural thoughts and remember that all is good, neither criticizing nor condemning people or things. We are spiritual only as far as we trust in the Spirit at all times, in all places, and under all conditions. In order to do this, we do not have to seclude ourselves from the world. To do so is an open confession of our own weakness and lack.

There are moments when it is best to be alone with the power. From these moments, we gather strength. To keep that strength to ourselves is pure selfishness. Walk, talk, live with the human race, hand in hand with all people and unified with all events. Live and love and learn. Be natural and normal. If you seek to enter some other way, you must do it all over again, for none live or die unto themselves, but unto all people.

THE CHURCH OF GOD

*   *   *

The church of God is not built with hands. It is eternal in the heavens. It is not lighted with candles. Its dome is heaven, and it is lighted by the stars of God's illumined thought. All members in their separate stars "shall draw the thing as they see it for the God of things as they are." Here, we recognize the God within our own souls. We ask for and see no other God. When we can look on all creation as the perfect work of a perfect God, we will become members of this church. When we can see the same person in the saint as we do in the sinner, when we realize that the one who kneels before the altar and the one who lies drunk in the street are the same one, when we love the one as much as we do the other, then we will be able to qualify.

As it now is, we have too many preachers who do not understand, who have no purpose. We have too many prayers, too many creeds, too many teachers who have no message, too many churches, too many "learned" people, and too few thinkers. "The realm of heaven comes not by observation." It is the still, small voice within the soul that speaks. The expanded thought will never wish to join or be joined to. Nothing human can contain it. It feels the limitation of form and ceremony. It longs for the freedom of the Spirit, the great out of doors, the great God of the everywhere. Alone in the desert, the forest, or by the restless ocean, looking up at the stars, humankind breathes forth these words, "With only my creator and me."

THE PATH TO PROSPERITY

* * *

The healing of conditions is no different from other healing. All healing is the constructive use of a mental law that the world is gradually beginning to understand something of. Again, we must reiterate the principle that we are surrounded by a thinking medium from which all things come. We think into it, and it does the rest. Since we are thinking beings, and since creative mind receives our thought and cannot stop creating, it must always be making something for us. What it makes depends absolutely and only on what we are thinking. What we will attract depends entirely on holding that thought to the complete exclusion of all that would contradict it. It is not enough that we should sit down and say, "I am one with infinite life." We must mean more than mere words. It must be felt. It must become an embodiment of a positive mental attitude. It is not claiming something to be true that is going to happen. It is not sending out an aspiration or a desire or a supplication or a prayer. It must be the embodiment of that which knows that now it *is*. This is more than holding a thought. Our ability to attract depends on the largeness of our thought as we feel that it flows out into a great universal creative power. We are dealing with the form in thought and not with the form in matter. We have learned that when we get the true form in thought and permeate it with the Spirit of belief, we will see the thought made flesh without any further effort on our part.

Thought can attract to us only that which we first mentally embody. We cannot attract to ourselves that which we are not. We can attract in the outer only that which we have first completely mentally embodied inside, that which has become a part of our mental makeup, a part of our inner understanding.

Those people going into business will attract to themselves that which they think about the most. If they cut hair, they will attract people who want to have their hair cut. If they sell shoes, they will attract people who want to buy shoes. So it is with everything. We will attract as much of anything as we mentally embody. This is apt to be overlooked in the study of spiritual philosophy. It is not enough to say that we attract what we think. We *become* what we think, and what we become, we will attract.

Do not become sentimental about this. Your life is governed by more than a sentiment. It is governed by law, something that cannot be broken, something that picks up every mental attitude and does something with it.

This fundamental proposition of the law will then work out into our conditions. Always remember that it does just as we think. It does not argue. It simply does the thing as we think it. So, how are we thinking? Never ask those for whom you pray how they are feeling. Instead, ask, "How are you thinking today?" This is the only thing that matters. How are we thinking about life and our conditions? Are we receiving the race suggestion? Are we saying that there is not enough to go around? If we are saying this, it is our belief, and there is something that will see that it becomes a part of our expression.

Most people, through ignorance of the higher laws of their being, are suffering from the thoughts imposed on them from a negative and doubtful world. We who claim the use of the greater law must emancipate ourselves from all sense of limitation. We are not to be governed by the outer confusion, but by the inner realization. We are to judge life not from the way that things in the past have been done, but from the way that the Spirit does things.

THE WAY OF THE SPIRIT

* * *

Again, the Spirit creates by becoming the thing that it thinks. There is no other possible way in which it could work. Since it is everything and there is no other, the thought of opposing forces never enters into its mental working.

When we judge from the outer, we are not working in line with the power that we should be using. We must come to see that there is only one power and that we are touching it at all points, because there is not a power of poverty and a power of prosperity. There is only the one becoming the many. It makes and it unmakes so that a higher form may appear to express through it. All that is not in line with its forward movement will soon pass away, because it recognizes no opposite. As far as we are concerned, what we are and what we are to become depends only on what we are thinking, because this is the way that we use creative power. The sooner we get away from the thought that we have to create, the sooner we will be able to work in line with the Spirit.

We never create anything; we only use. The united intelligence of the human race could not make a single rosebud; it does not know enough. But our slightest thought adrift in mind causes the same power that makes all things to create for us.

The great error of the race is, and always has been, that we give a physical reason for things. When that reason has not answered the problems of life, we have sought out some other reason just as physical. The fact that we are wrong is shown in that every generation has found a different reason. When truth is found, it will also be found that it never changes to suit the whims of the human fancy. This is proven by the fact that the real truth the race has discovered has never been changed.

The truth that was revealed to the prophets of old has never changed. It is the same today as it was thousands of years ago. Whoever touches truth, no matter in what generation, will always get the same answer. The great truth that was revealed from Moses to the time of Jesus is the same truth that is still revealed to all who will accept it. It is simply this: We are now living in a spiritual universe governed by mental laws of cause and effect. Moses saw it mostly from the standpoint of the law of cause and effect, an eye for an eye. What does this mean? It means, as Jesus said, "As one sows, so shall one reap." Moses saw the law.

Jesus saw not only the law ("I am come not to destroy, but to fulfill"), but he also saw the reason behind the law. He revealed the great lawgiver behind all law, a God of love working out the great inner concepts of its own being in harmony and in beauty, filled with peace, causing the sun to shine on the just and the unjust alike. Jesus did not try to overcome the use of law. He understood all law, and he knew that all law was at his command. He did not break the law; he fulfilled it. So we must find that everything is at our command through these same laws. Those who understand law and comply with it will have no difficulty in demonstrating that it is as true for them as it ever was for anyone else.

What, then, are the laws underlying prosperity? The first is this, and we must not try to escape it: "You shall have no other Gods before me." This "me" is Spirit. We are, then, to trust only in the activity of Spirit for what we need. But the world will say, "Human things come through human agencies." This may be true, but we must realize that the power we are dealing with also has within its own mind all people and all things. We do not have to pray for people; we have to embody principle. Principle may use people, but that is not part of our responsibility.

Ultimately, everything is Spirit, and Spirit, which is the beginning, is also the end of all manifestation. "I am the alpha and the omega." Our life, then, is to be governed by Spirit. We need look no further. It will do for us all that we will ever ask, provided we believe. Why, then, has it not done so? The answer is that it has already done so, but we have not received it. The Spirit may offer, but we must accept the gift before it can be made. "Behold, I stand at the door and knock." We must understand that this receiving is a mental process. It is one of mentally receiving.

The way, then, that we use mind through our thought is the way that we pray for prosperity. So simple, and yet we have not understood it. If we say, "I have not," we will not receive. If we say, "I have," we will receive. "To those who have shall be given, and to those who have not shall be taken away even that which they have." This is a veiled statement of the law of cause and effect.

When we send out into mind the thought that we have not, it accepts the idea and takes away from us even that which we have. Reverse the process and say, "I have," and it will at once set to work to create for us even more than we now possess. We will readily see then that we are not dealing with two powers, but with one, and that it operates through our own thought, doing unto us even as we believe.

THE LEVEL OF CONSCIOUSNESS

* * *

Since all is mind, and it is done unto us as we mentally think, all life is simply a law of thought, an activity of consciousness. In our life, the power flows through us. If we provide a big receptivity, it will do a big thing; if we only believe in a small way, the activity must be a small one. The Spirit can do for us only what it can do through us. Unless we are able to provide the consciousness, it cannot make the gift.

Few people have a great consciousness, and this ex-plains why so few excel. The power behind all things is of itself without limit; it is all-power. In us, it has to become what we make it. We carry within our own soul the key to all expression, but few of us use it. The door is not seen with the physical eye, and until now only a few have gained the ability to see. The majority of us merely look. Realizing, then, that the power is limitless and must become operative through our own thought, we see that what we need is not some greater power, but that what we really need is a greater consciousness, a deeper realization of life, a grander concept of being. We must unify ourselves with the great whole.

Those who dare to fling their thoughts out into universal intelligence with the positive assurance of one who knows and dares to claim all there is will find that it will be done. God will honor their requests. On the other hand, those who fear to speak lest God smites them will find themselves smitten of the law, not because God is angry, but because it is done as we believe.

We have a right to have—and should expect to have—in this world all that will make for comfort and for the luxuries of life. It does not matter how much we have as long as we rob no other soul to get it. The power that so lavishly spreads itself out into nature gives to us its highest expression. We dishonor God when we claim less than all. Until we expand our thought so that we are able to say "I am," we should not expect to get great results.

The soul that knows its own divinity is the great soul. Before it, all else must bend, and to it, all else must gravitate. Enlarge your thought process. Do away with the personal thoughts of little things, and dare to think in universal terms about all things.

The universe is running over with good. It is for you, but you must believe and then take it. Do you dare to believe that your own word is invincible? When you speak it, how do you feel? Is it limitless? Is it all power? Is all power given to you in heaven and on earth? Are you one with the only power that there is? Until you can say "yes" to all these questions, not simply believing it, but knowing it, you cannot hope to attain. It is useless to beg for things when you do prayer work. It is like begging for water to be wet or fire to be hot. Things simply are; we must take them. Your word has only the power that you put into it, no more and no less.

We are each held accountable for every word that we speak, because all is the action and the reaction of mind. We are each our own heaven and our own hell. If we start a new venture and question our chances of success, we have not realized that the outer is simply the inner manifested. When we go to a new place, we will find there only that which we have taken with us. If we have taken success, we will find success; if we have taken failure, we will find failure. This is the law. No one can avoid it, and no one should try. Every living soul is a law unto that soul's own life. "There is no law but my own soul shall set." Nothing can come upon the path of the soul except that thing that the soul attracts.

PRACTICE FOR PROSPERITY

* * *

Prosperity is in our own hands to do with as we will, but we will never reach it until we learn to control our thought. We must see only what we want and never allow the other things to enter. If we wish activity, we must be active in our thought. We must see activity and speak it into everything that we do. The spoken word will bring it to pass. We speak the word, and it is brought to pass of the power that we speak it into.

We can only speak the word that we understand. The activity will correspond to our inner concepts. If it is large, the results will be large. The thing to do is to unify ourselves with all the biggest ideas that we can encompass. Realizing that our ideas govern our power of attraction, we should be constantly enlarging within ourselves. We must realize our *at-one-ment* with all power and know that our word will bring it to pass. We speak the word, and it is brought to pass. As consciousness grows, it will manifest in enlarged opportunities and a greater field of action. Most people think in the terms of universal powers. When you speak, feel that you are surrounded by all the power that there is and never doubt that what you say will spring into being.

We should speak into mind all that we desire and believe that it will be done unto us. Never take the time to listen to those who doubt. Their philosophy has done little to save the world or themselves. Here again, let the dead bury the dead, and see to it that you maintain what you want in your own thought, letting go of all else. Think only what you want to happen, and never let yourself get mentally lazy and sluggish taking on the suggestions of poverty and limitation. See yourself as being in the position that you desire. Mentally dwell on it, and speak with perfect assurance that it is done. Then, forget it and trust in the law. This will answer all needs. If you want to do this for someone else, all that you need to do is to think of them and go through the same process of mental action. You will be sending out the truth for them, and mind, being always active, will not contradict what you have said.

You cannot hope to get results unless you keep only the one idea and do not mix thoughts in your mind. Everything is yours, but you must take it. The taking is always a mental process. It is believing absolutely. This is divine principle.

Conclusion

* * *

Principle itself is simplicity, yet it is infinite. It is infinite mind and manifestation of mind. We live in a spiritual universe governed through the thought, or the word, that first becomes law. This law creates matter.

Jesus discerned the truth about spiritual principles more than any other person who ever lived, and he proclaimed the eternal dominion of law and understanding, absolute, complete, perfect. He found the law to be operative through his own thought and the power of his own word. When you and I stop looking outside ourselves to any person and realize that whatever truth and power we have must flow through us, when we begin to interpret our own natures, then we will begin to understand God, law, and life, and not until then.

We live, move, and have our being in an infinite, creative mind that is infinitely receptive, operative, omnipotent, and all-knowing. We have learned that this mind presses against us on all sides, flows through us, and becomes operative through our thinking. The human race, ignorant of the laws of this mind, ignorant of the power of its own thought, has, through its ignorance, misused and abused the creative power of its thought and brought on itself the thing it feared. This is true because all thought is law and all law is mind in action, and the word that you speak today is the law that governs your life tomorrow, just as the word you spoke yesterday, whether ignorantly or innocently, consciously or unconsciously, is absolutely governing your life today.

As students of spiritual philosophy, then, we are neither dealing with nor denying a manifest universe, but we are claiming that the manifestation is the result of the inner activity of the mind. If we wish for a definite manifestation, we must produce a definite inner activity. You and I, then, are not dealing with conditions, but with mental and spiritual law. We are dealing with the power of thought, the power of mind, and the more spiritual the thought, the higher the manifestation. The more our reliance on God, the greater the power.

This is the new education, because it strips all the false

from the old belief and reveals the individual. It is the new age, because as sure as God is, God will usher in and express the perfect life, the revelation of this truth, and our ability to use it. It is our own fault when we know this and do not prove it.

If, knowing the infinite power flowing through you, you still remain sick and unhappy, miserable and poor, it is your own fault. Do not blame God, do not blame others, and do not say it is of the devil. It is your own fault. Every time you say "I am," you are recognizing the eternal, infinite presence of omnipotent power within yourself, which is God operating through your thought, and that is why you bring upon yourself the thing you fear and why you bring to yourself the thing you want.

On that day when at least fifty-one percent of your thinking is health and life and power, then that fifty-one percent will swallow up, erase, and kill the rest. The day you as an individual, using at least fifty-one percent of your thought, pass beyond the perception of limitation, you will draw out of the universe everything you desire. Poverty will desert you, and you will be emancipated forever. The day you think at least fifty-one percent of happiness, misery will depart and never return. The journey is worth your time and effort. The greatest purpose in the life of any awakened soul is to depict this principle and emancipate itself.

The way can be shown, but it is up to each person to walk the way. We are so bound by suggestion and hypnotized by false belief, so entangled by the chaotic thinking of the world, thinking that is based on the principle of a dual mind, that we become confused and are not ourselves. Wake up! Your word is all-powerful. Your consciousness is one with omnipotence. Your thought is infinite. Your destiny is eternal, and your home is everlasting heaven. Realize this truth: I am living in a perfect universe. It always was perfect and always will be perfect. There never was a mistake made. There are no mistakes being made and there never will be. You live in the great and eternal universe of perfection from cause to effect, from beginning to end, and "the world's all right, and I know it."

Majestic and calm, waiting with eternal and divine patience, the great principle of life is ready to give to us all that it has. And while we listen and wait, we will cast from us everything that hinders its complete expression through us. We will let go of all struggle and all strife and be at peace with life.

Perfect peace to the soul rests in the realization of its unity with all that there is, was, or ever will be. One with the infinite mind. All the power of the Spirit is working through our thought as we believe and receive.

Now we will ask for and take the thing that we desire.

It is done. It is complete, now and forever. Perfect life, perfect healing, perfect harmony, divine guidance, infinite strength, and joy forever.

QUESTIONS AND ANSWERS

* * *

What is the truth?

Truth is that which is. It is all that is. Just as there cannot be something and nothing, so the truth, being that which is, must at the same time be all that there is.

Where is the truth?

If the truth is everything, it must be everywhere. Being all, there is no other substance to divide it with. Being undivided, it is present everywhere. All truth, which means all power, must be present at all points or at any given point at any and all times.

Has the truth changed?

A substance cannot change unless there is something for it to change into. Since the truth is all, it cannot change because there is no other thing for it to change into. The truth, then, has never changed.

Is the truth one or many?

It must be one, since it is all.

Is the truth conscious?

Yes, because humankind is conscious. It could not be so unless truth, or life, was conscious. Humankind's self-consciousness proves the self-consciousness of life, truth, and Spirit. Like produces like.

What comes out of life?

Everything that exists comes out of life. If life is all there is, then it follows that everything is some form of life.

How does life make things?

Being all, it must make things out of itself. It must operate on itself through itself, and out of itself must make all that is made. Being conscious, it must know that it is doing this.

What would we call this inner movement of life?

The inner movement of life, or consciousness, we would call thought, or the self-knowing of life, or Spirit.

Then the universe and all that is a part of it comes from thought?

Yes, everything comes from thought.

Do we not see a visible world that seems to change? And if we do, how is it that it could come from something that never changes?

Yes, we do see a changing world, but behind it is a changeless substance. The thing that changes is the thought, or form. The substance from which this form comes never changes. It is one and undivided and takes form through thought in all things. We prove this when we resolve all things into one source. All material things can be reduced to formless substance, the sole activity of which must be thought or the movement of intelligence upon itself.

What causes form to change?

The intelligence behind it.

Is there nothing in the universe but life, thought, and form?

These are all.

If this is true, what is physical law?

Physical law is simply the result of the inner movement of life.

If things and laws are the result of the inner movement of life, then does it not follow that thoughts are things?

Yes, all things are simply thought forms.

How long does thought last as form?

As long as the thought is held in life, or mind.

Does the thought of life, mind, or good ever change?

From all that we can know, the thought of God does seem to change. Planets change, take form, and again become formless. When we realize that all this can take place without ever changing the substance behind it, we see no reason why God's thought could not change and continually build up a higher form. Indeed, this is one of the teachings of ancient wisdom, that while reality never changes, the form that it takes is always changing.

What is humankind's place in the creative order?

Humankind is a thinking center in mind, reproducing in a smaller scale all that there is in the universe.

Does this not make humankind's thought creative?

In a certain sense it does. Creation is not making something out of nothing; it is thought taking form. As one thinks and as thought must take form, it must follow that one's thought must take form in mind and become creative.

What is humankind's thought?

It is the activity of that something within that can say, "I am."

What is the difference between God and the individual?

The very fact that we can say "I am" proves that we are. Since we are, we must be made out of life and must be some part of all that there is. This being so, the individual must be a part of God's consciousness. The difference would be in degree only. The individual must be as much of life as it recognizes itself to be.

Is all of our thought creative?

Yes, all or none. If one thought produces, then all must.

If this is true, why do we seem to be so limited?

Because we have thought limitation. Thoughts are things and will always make the thing thought of. In reality, the very fact that our thought limits us also proves that we could free ourselves from limitation by changing our thoughts.

Why are we made so that we can think two ways?

This is a question that can be answered only in one way. Unless we could think as we want to think, we would not be human at all, but merely pieces of a machine. We are individuals, and that means we possess self-choice backed by a power that will produce the thing chosen. In discovering ourselves, we choose many things, use them, and pass to a higher choice, always ascending in the scale of being. As fast as we choose, we experience the thing that we think about.

What is evil?

Evil is the result of a lack of clear observation based on a belief in two powers and limitation. What we call *sin* is the result of humankind's struggle to find itself.

If this is true, why could we not at once begin to change our whole life by first changing our thought?

We could. We would not be changing real substance, but we would be changing the form that it takes through our thought. All that we can change is the form of thought through which experiences come to us.

What is the limit of our creative use of mind?

We are limited by nothing except our own thinking, by our mental ability to conceive.

What is meant by mental conception?

All things are produced by thought. The thing produced from mind is first formed in thought. Thought molds mind into form.

But do we not have to act?

We cannot think without acting. An inactive body is the result of an inactive mind.

In using our creative powers, how far do we have to consider the conditions under which we live?

We do not have to consider them at all. Conditions are the result, the effect, and not the cause. We create conditions as quickly as we think.

How would we start to change conditions?

By first changing thought and by realizing that we are not dealing with an illusion, but with the great reality. Then, by acting as though we already have what we think.

How long would it take to do this?

As long as it would take to let go of all negative

thought and embody all positive thought. This would depend entirely on the individual and the individual's mental ability to control thought.

What would hinder us the most?

Ourselves. No one gives to us except ourselves, and no one takes from us except ourselves.

Can no one else help us?

Only to a limited degree. While we may be helped for a time by those who understand the law, sooner or later we must ourselves take the creative responsibility of our own lives. Others may think for us for a few moments a day, but we think for ourselves all the time.

But doesn't God help us?

Yes, God helps everyone, but God must do it through law. "All's love, yet all's law."

How should we pray?

By giving thanks that we already have the thing that we pray for. By completely believing and never doubting. "When you pray, believe that you have received, and you shall receive." We must be sure that in no way do we think, act, talk, or read about limitation. We must all be a law unto ourselves.

Definitions

* * *

God—Infinite Spirit, self-knowing mind, life, truth, intelligence, love, all cause and all effect. The invisible power that makes all things out of itself by an inner action of its own thought upon itself.

The visible universe—The ideas of God in expression, the body of God, expression of the divine mind. All visible life is an expression of an inner concept.

Law—Mind in action. Law is not cause; it is effect. It is intelligence operating. All law is universal.

Vibration—Not intelligence, but the result of intelligence. It follows cause.

Thought—The activity of mind.

Humankind—A thinking center in mind.

Creation—Thought becoming form. The immaculate conception.

Sin—Lack of understanding.

Righteousness—Spiritual understanding.

Sickness—Image of thought held in mind appearing on the body.

Health—The realization of perfect life.

Poverty—Limited thought.

Riches—The realization of our unity with life, which is limitless.

Consciousness—The realization of the fact that we are.

Life—Consciousness of power and activity.

Truth—That which is.

Realization—An inner thought process whereby we become conscious of our unity with life.

Absolute—Complete self-knowing.

Causation—God, Spirit, life, that which is.

Intelligence—That which knows that it is.

Unfoldment—The birth of ideas coming forth from mind.

Illusion—Belief in two powers.

Soul—The inner creative life, the receptive, creativity.

Sense—Not an illusion, but the faculties through which we contact life in its expression.

Motion—The inner activity of life producing manifestation.

Effect—The result of inner motion.

Word—The activity of thought.

Faith—Positive mental activity.

Fear—Negative mental activity.

Attraction—The drawing power of thought.

Unity—One mind flowing through all and in all.

Objective—Life in its outer form.

Subjective—Life in its inner thought or form.

Karma—The law of cause and effect. The result of past thought and action binding the ignorant and freeing the wise.

Multiplicity—The bringing forth from the one of an infinite variety of form, color, and motion.

Affirmative prayer—The mental and spiritual activity of thought for a definite end.

Demonstration—The result of correct thinking.

Heaven—The atmosphere of correct thought.

Hell—The atmosphere of false thinking.

Peace—Mind resting in the realization that it is all.

Poise—An inner calm that never fears.

Power—The result of the union of peace and poise.

ABOUT THE AUTHOR

Ernest Shurtleff Holmes (1887–1960), an ordained Divine Science minister, was founder of a spiritual movement known as Religious Science, a part of the New Thought movement, whose spiritual philosophy is known as Science of Mind. He was the author of *The Science of Mind* and numerous other metaphysical books, as well as founder of *Science of Mind* magazine, in continuous publication since 1927.

*If you enjoyed Ernest Holmes' Creative Mind,
you may enjoy these other fine Newt List titles.*

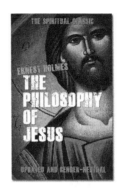

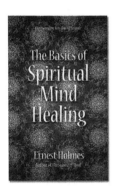

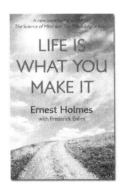

www.NewtList.com

Original editions of classic books, such as *Creative Mind,* written by Ernest Holmes in 1919, hold great value as documents that not only give us the information we want, but do so in a way that imparts a sense of the time in which they were written, through language usage, idiom, even punctuation. Yet there is value in revising and updating book manuscripts from the past. With skilled editing, new editions of classic books can invigorate the manuscript and clear up language that can be challenging to understand today, while at the same time, retain the author's distinctive voice and intention. Such is the case with the books of Newt List.

Newt List offers updated editions of spiritual classic texts. Newt List titles have been edited to provide contemporary language structure and idioms that have evolved since the original manuscript was published. We revise punctuation and capitalizations, and adjust sentence structure when appropriate, as well as update certain words or terms that have since become obscure, as long as those changes do not affect the author's intention or expression.

More valuable for readers today, though, is Newt List's procedure of updating gender forms. In the time of original publication, these classic books generally used masculine forms when referring to God or humankind. Newt List edits all its books using gender-neutral language, making the ideas in them apply more broadly to all readers.

If you have never read these amazing books in their original editions, you are in for a great adventure—a new way of thinking about life. If you *have* read these books before, Newt List thinks you will find that our books come alive in original and fresh ways which make the ideas in them more immediate, relevant, and, more importantly, life changing.

For more books by Ernest Holmes
and other New Thought authors,
visit NewtList.com.

89825645R00105

Made in the USA
San Bernardino, CA
04 October 2018